Merry Christmas 1981

With love,

Mommy & Daddy

Winnie-the-Pooh

GALLERY BOOKS
An imprint of W.H. Smith Publishers Inc.
112 Madison Avenue
New York, New York 10016

A Bison Book

One fine autumn day, Winnie-the-Pooh sat on a log in front of his house. Something seemed to be wrong. Instead of his usual smile, Pooh Bear was wearing a frown. Whatever could be the matter?

Aha! But there's the answer. Beside him lay four honey jars — all of them empty. And Pooh was very hungry.

"Oh bother! I can't have finished all the honey," said Winnie-the-Pooh, scratching his head and wandering back inside the house.

Noisely pulling everything out of the cupboard, he stuck his paw into one of the jars. "There's a bit left in this one, but hardly enough for a hungry bear like me," said Pooh as he licked his paw.

Just then he heard a buzzing sound. Turning around, he saw a bee fly in through the window.

"A bee," thought Winnie-the-Pooh. "Now what do bees do? They make honey. And the only reason for making honey is so I can eat it!" Shouting with joy, he followed the bee outside. The bee flew up into a tall tree.

"Now, if I can just follow that bee, he's bound to lead me to honey," said Winnie-the-Pooh as he began climbing the tree. Finally, Pooh reached the spot where the bee had disappeared. But just as he was about to stick his paw into the hole, the branch he was standing on broke and Winnie-the-Pooh went crashing down.

"Oops! Ouch!" squeaked
Pooh, as he tumbled from
branch to branch. Splosh!
Winnie-the-Pooh landed in a
mud puddle.

"This would never have
happened if I didn't like
honey so much," he sighed
as he landed in a mud
puddle.

Not far away, at the edge of the forest, lived
Christopher Robin. He was a good friend to all the
animals. Always willing to lend a hand, that day he was
busy helping out poor Eeyore, the donkey, who had lost
his tail.

"Now Eeyore, I'm going to nail your tail back on. Try
not to lose it again," said Christopher Robin, as he
knelt down behind the donkey. Watching were Owl and
Kanga.

"A bit to the left," said Kanga.

"No, absolutely not," said Owl. "Move it to the right."
When Christopher Robin had finished, Eeyore gave his
tail a mighty swish.

"Thanks," he brayed. "It's just an old tail, but I'm
kind of attached to it."

Just as the animals and Christopher Robin were congratulating each other, along came Winnie-the-Pooh.

"Hello, Pooh, what have you been up to now?" asked Christopher Robin, looking at the muddy bear.

"Hello, Christopher Robin, I was just wondering, uh, just thinking about whether you had such a thing as a balloon?"

"What do you want a balloon for?" asked Christopher Robin.

Winnie-the-Pooh looked around and whispered, "honey."

"But you don't get honey with a balloon," pointed out the puzzled Christopher Robin.

"I do," insisted Pooh Bear, and started to roll over and over in a mud puddle until he was completely coated. Then he took the balloon from Christopher Robin and began floating slowly upward.

"I'll be able to reach the bee's nest with this," he explained.

"But the bees will see you," shouted Christopher Robin.

"No they won't. With this mud all over me, they'll think I'm a little black rain cloud," laughed Winnie-the-Pooh as he floated higher and higher.

Christopher Robin followed along below, as the breeze blew Pooh Bear back towards the honey tree. When he was close enough to the hole, he stuck in his paw and pulled out a glob of honey.

"Yum! Yum! Yum! Nothing like fresh honey," said Pooh, dripping honey everywhere. A swarm of angry bees flew out of the nest and buzzed threateningly around him.

"Christopher Robin," squealed Winnie-the-Pooh. "I think the bees suspect something."

"They probably think that you're after their honey!" shouted back Christopher Robin.

By this time there were lots of bees buzzing angrily around Winnie-the-Pooh.

"Christopher Robin. I have come to the conclusion that these are not the right sort of bees," said Pooh, slapping away the angry bees. "No, not at all a nice sort of bee," he said, as a bee stung his nose.

With Pooh perched precariously on top of the drifting balloon, the swarm of bees suddenly attacked and there was a loud hissing noise. Air was escaping from the balloon.

"Christopher Robin!" called Winnie-the-Pooh, "I think I will come down now."

"Don't worry, Pooh." And running over with outstretched arms Christopher Robin caught the bear just as he landed.

"Oh dear," sighed Winnie-the-Pooh. "If only I didn't like honey so much."

Winnie-the-Pooh wasn't one to give up easily. No sooner were his bee stings better than he had another idea.

"Honey — that rhymes with — bunny." "I think I'll go pay Rabbit a visit."

Rabbit was just about to pour himself a cup of tea when Pooh popped his head around the corner and shouted, "Anybody at home?"

The startled rabbit spilled his tea. "Oh, no. Not Pooh," he thought in alarm. "He'll eat me out of house and home."

"Hello, Pooh. What a pleasant surprise. How about lunch?" said Rabbit.

"Thank you Rabbit. I am feeling a bit hungry," said Pooh, sitting down at the table.

Rabbit brought out a jar of honey. "Would you like some honey on your bread?" he asked.

"Don't bother about the bread. I'll just take a tiny helping of honey," said Winnie, tying a napkin around his neck.

Rabbit poured out a small helping of honey. Pooh looked down at the tiny blob of honey. "What's wrong?" asked Rabbit.

"Well," said Pooh, "I did mean a somewhat larger tiny helping."

"Perhaps you should just help yourself." said Rabbit, handing him the jar.

Winnie began eating honey from the jar. He soon finished that jar and started on another. He ate and ate and ate until he was practically covered in honey. Licking his paws, he turned to Rabbit and said, "Thanks so much. I think I'll be going now."

Rabbit looked at the bloated bear. "You're sure you won't have anymore?"

"It there anymore?" asked Pooh, looking around at the empty jars.

"No, there isn't," said the rabbit, shaking Pooh's sticky paw.

Still licking his paws, Pooh started to leave. Suddenly, Rabbit heard a muffled shout. "Oh, help! I'm stuck." Pooh Bear was wedged in the doorway.

"That's what happens when you eat too much," said the rabbit, pushing Pooh from behind.

"No," said Pooh. "This is what happens when you make your door too small."

All Rabbit's pushing and Pooh's struggling just made things worse.

Pooh Bear was wedged in the doorway so tightly that he didn't budge an inch. Finally Pooh started to yell for help. Soon Owl arrived. "Well, if it isn't Winnie-the-Pooh!"

"Hello, Owl," replied Pooh.

"Are you by any chance stuck?" asked Owl.

"Oh, no. Just resting and thinking, that's all," grumbled the irritated bear.

"Yes, I'd say you were most definitely in a tight spot," said Owl as he took a closer look.

Back inside his house, Rabbit was staring at Pooh's rear end. "Oh dear. Oh gracious. If I have to look at that — that thing for some time, I might as well make the best of it," he muttered.

Rabbit placed branches on either side of Pooh's rear and put a frame around it.

"A hunting trophy!" exclaimed the rabbit, stepping back to admire his work.

That night Pooh was still wedged in the hole when along came a gopher. "I hear there's an excavation problem here. My name's Gopher and here's my card. What's the problem?"

"I'm the problem," said Winnie. "I'm stuck in this doorway."

Gopher dusted off Winnie and tied a scarf around his head. "Looks as if this may take several days," he said, opening his lunch box.

"Several days!" yelled Winnie. "What about meals?"

"Oh, no thanks. I've brought mine with me," said the gopher and began to eat.

Later that night, Gopher saw that it would be very difficult indeed to unwedge Pooh. Staying only long enough to eat up the last few crumbs of his food, the gopher packed up and left.

"Oh dear," yawned Pooh Bear. "If only I didn't like honey so much, this never would have happened."

When Christopher Robin was told of Pooh Bear's predicament he came running to help his friend. After much thought, Christopher decided that the only solution was to wait until Winnie-the-Pooh lost weight.

"We're going to put you on a diet, Pooh," said Christopher Robin. "And a diet means NO HONEY!" he declared firmly.

Finally one day, as Rabbit was beginning to despair of ever using his front door again, Pooh began to budge. Christopher Robin, Kanga and Eeyore tugged on Pooh from outside, while Rabbit pushed from the inside.

And with a hearty heave-ho Pooh was free at last.

Several days later, as Winnie-the-Pooh strolled through the forest, a great wind lifted him off his feet.

"Oh goodness! I must have lost a lot of weight — I feel as light as a feather," said the surprised bear. And like a feather, Winnie-the-Pooh was swept up through the woods.

A storm was brewing and
the wind became even
stronger.

Pooh thought he heard a
familiar voice, and looking
ahead saw his friend Piglet.

"Piglet! You, too! Wait for
me," shouted Pooh, as he
reached out and grabbed
Piglet's scarf.

Just then a wind separated the two friends. Pooh Bear went flying up towards the tree where Owl lived while Piglet clung onto a branch with all his might.

Owl poked his head out of the door. "Nice of you to drop in, Winnie-the-Pooh," he said. "Oh, and I see you've brought Piglet with you. Well, do come in."

Seated in Owl's house, Pooh and Piglet had the sensation that the house was swaying. Owl, in his rocking chair, didn't seem to notice.

"I say, Owl," said Winnie-the-Pooh. "The house appears to be moving."

"Nonsense," declared Owl. "This house is as solid as a rock. It'll take more than a little breeze to blow it away."

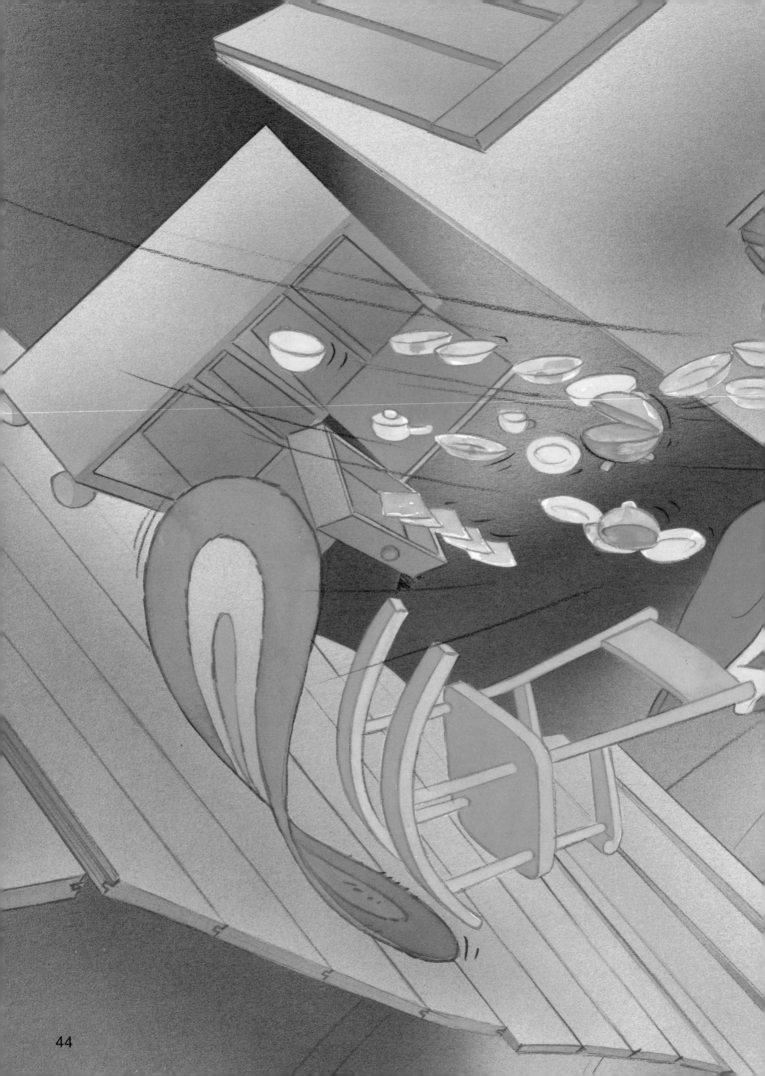

But no sooner had Owl said this than an enormous gust of wind blew the roof off. The cupboard doors flew open and plates and saucers came tumbling out. Before anyone could say a word, Winnie-the-Pooh, Piglet and Owl were all blown out of the house.

As soon as the storm was over, Pooh found his way home and hopped into his warm snuggly bed. But in the middle of the night he was awoken by a very strange noise. Peeking out from beneath his blankets, Pooh listened intently.

After a while, gathering up his courage and his pop gun, Pooh Bear crept to the door.

Winnie-the-Pooh opened the door and peered cautiously out. He couldn't see anything. But then, before he knew what had hit him, a tiger jumped on the frightened bear, knocking him over.

"Hello! I'm Tigger," said the tiger looking down at Pooh. "That's spelled T I double G RRR. Tigger. What's your name?"

"My name is Winnie-the-Pooh and you scared me," said the astonished Pooh.

"Of course I scared you. Tiggers are meant to be scary," replied the tiger, who wasn't really very frightening, after all.

Tigger bounced off Pooh and began to look around the house. Stopping in front of the mirror he asked, "What's that?"

"It's a tiger. I mean it's you, silly," said Pooh. "A tiger in striped pajamas! You must be joking," laughed Tigger. "I'll teach that tiger to laugh at me," he added and he began to growl at the tiger in the mirror. But when the tiger in the mirror growled back, Tigger became frightened and bounced out of the house.

This was too much for Pooh Bear, who was beginning to wonder if he was dreaming. He was very tired and soon slumped to the floor, fast asleep.

While Winnie-the-Pooh dreamed of honey and other nice things, a heavy rain began to fall.

Pooh's nice dream began to turn into a nightmare. He dreamed that he was being drowned in honey.

Suddenly Pooh Bear awoke and found himself in a puddle, but not of honey. There was water everywhere.

"Oh, no! My honey!" yelled Pooh. "I musn't let the water get into my honey jars."

Within a few minutes
Pooh had carried all of his
precious reserves of honey to
safety up in the big tree
above his house.

The rain continued to fall
in torrents and the forest
became a vast lake.

All the climbing up and down had made Pooh a bit hungry. "I'll just have a little snack," he said as he poked his nose into one of the jars.

While Pooh was busy eating honey, the water continued to rise until it touched the branch where the bear stood.

A sudden wave of water knocked Pooh over headfirst into the honey jar. With his legs kicking in the air, he made quite a sight floating in the water.

Nearby was Piglet, who had wisely jumped onto a kitchen chair. "Is that you, Winnie-the-Pooh?" shouted Piglet. "It's me, Piglet. Can you hear me?"

Piglet was too busy trying to get Pooh's attention to notice the waterfall up ahead. Both Pooh and Piglet cried out in alarm, but there was nothing they could do. They reached the roaring waterfall and plunged downward, tumbling over and over as they were thrown about by the falling water. When they landed in the pool below, Pooh was on the kitchen chair and Piglet was in the honey jar.

Luckily, Christopher Robin had been on the look-out for his little friends and he soon had the water-logged bear and piglet safe on land.

Once the flood waters had receded, Christopher Robin decided to have a party. He invited Rabbit, Kanga and little Roo, Piglet, Pooh and Tigger too.

Owl stood on his chair and made a speech about the brave Piglet and Winnie-the-Pooh.

Everything seemed to be back to normal — at least, for the moment.

Several weeks later, while Rabbit was picking carrots in his garden, Tigger decided to bounce by.

"Oh, no!" groaned Rabbit when he saw Tigger bouncing in his cabbage patch. With every bounce, Tigger managed to create havoc — even cabbages were scattered and squashed.

"Hello Rabbit!" shouted Tigger.

Rabbit looked around at the scattered vegetables. "Just look at what you've done to my beautiful garden," he shouted, waving his fist.

"Yuck! Messy isn't it?" said Tigger, examining the destruction.

"You've ruined it, Tigger. It's your doing. You and your confounded bouncing! When are you going to stop all that bouncing?" demanded the angry Rabbit.

As Tigger bounced about, Rabbit turned to Piglet and Winnie-the-Pooh.

"I'm going to teach that Tigger a lesson," he said. "Let's take him for a long walk in the forest — and then lose him."

"Lose him?" asked Pooh.

"Not forever. Just long enough to take some of that bounce out of him," replied Rabbit.

The next morning the little group set off into the forest. As usual, Tigger bounced ahead of everyone.

After a while, the three friends managed to lose Tigger, who bounced off into the misty forest. After waiting some time to be sure that Tigger was truly out of sight, Rabbit nudged the others and they turned towards home. However, the mist had thickened, making everything look different.

"You know, Rabbit," said Winnie-the-Pooh. "I don't think we lost Tigger. I think he lost us."

And so it was that the lesson Rabbit wanted to teach Tigger backfired.

When the first snowfall covered the woods where the animals lived, little Roo was anxiously waiting for Tigger to come and take him out to play.

"Now you be careful," said Roo's mother, Mrs Kanga, when Tigger arrived. "Do bring Roo back before it gets dark," she shouted, as Tigger and Roo bounced off to play.

Tigger and Roo reached the frozen pond.

"Can you ice skate, Tigger?" asked Roo.

"Can Tigger ice skate? Why, that's what a Tigger does best — aside from bouncing, of course," said Tigger as he glided over the ice.

Soon Tigger was doing figures of eight and skating backwards, while Roo cheered him on.

Tigger began doing spins and other fancy moves. He was so absorbed in showing-off that he didn't see Rabbit in front of him.

"Oh, no. Not you!" shouted Rabbit, as Tigger came spinning towards him.

"Look out!" shouted Tigger. "Out of my way. I can't —" Tigger screamed, as he banged into Rabbit, "stop."

Leaving Rabbit sprawled out on the ice, Tigger took Roo on his shoulder and bounced into the woods.

"Can you climb a tree, Tigger?" asked Roo.

"Climb a tree! Why that's what Tiggers do best. Only I don't climb trees — I bounce them."

With Roo still proudly sitting on his shoulder, Tigger bounced from limb to limb of a tall tree. Higher and higher he bounced, until he could go no further.

The last bounce was too much for Roo, who fell off Tigger's shoulder. On the way down, Roo grabbed onto the tiger's tail. The little kangaroo began to swing back and forth, "This is fun," he shouted. "I've never swung on a tiger tail before."

"Hey! Stop that, please. You're rocking the forest," said Tigger, as the tree began to sway dangerously.

Roo let go of Tigger's tail and landed on a branch below. "What's wrong Tigger?" he asked.

"Oh, thank goodness. I was getting seasick," replied Tigger.

Just then, Tigger spotted Piglet and Pooh.

"HELLLLOOO!" shouted the tiger.

"Why it's Tigger and Roo," said Winnie-the-Pooh.

"What are you two doing up there?" shouted the bear.

"We bounced up. But now Tigger is stuck," said Roo.

Mrs Kanga and Rabbit came
over to see what all the
shouting was about.

"Oh, dear" exclaimed
Mrs Kanga. "Well, do be
careful. Jump into my
apron. I'll catch you," said
Mrs Kanga, as she got ready
to catch Roo.

"Weeee! That was fun,"
said Roo, leaping down and
landing in his mother's
apron.

"Okay, you're next!" Pooh and Rabbit shouted to Tigger. "Jump!"

"Jump? Tiggers don't jump — they bounce," said Tigger, grabbing tightly onto the tree.

"Then bounce down!" shouted Pooh.

"Don't be ridiculous," said Tigger. "Tiggers don't bounce down — they bounce up!"

"Then climb down!" shouted Rabbit.

"Tiggers don't climb down — because, because — their tails get in the way,"replied Tigger, wrapping his tail around the tree.

"That settles it. If he won't jump or climb down he'll have to stay up there forever," yelled Rabbit, who was rather enjoying this.

"Forever?" yelled Tigger. "I promise if I ever get out of this I'll never bounce again. Never!"

"Did you hear that, everyone?" asked Rabbit gleefully. "He promised. He said never." shouted Rabbit.

The animals decided that the best way to get Tigger down was to tell him to slide. And so, ever so slowly and ever so cautiously, Tigger slid down the tree.

"Tigger, you can open your eyes now. You're safe," said Piglet, as Tigger reached the bottom of the tree.

Tigger was so happy to be back on the ground that he began to kiss the snow. "I'm so happy, I feel like bouncing!" he said and with that he began to bounce.

"Wait a minute. You promised, Tigger," said Rabbit.

Tigger sat down. "Oh, I did, didn't I? You mean I can never bounce again?"

Rabbit and the others shook their heads. Tigger sighed, and slunk sadly over to a nearby log. There was a long silence.

"I like the old bouncy Tigger best," said Piglet finally.

"So do I. So do I," replied Kanga and Roo quickly.

"Of course, we all do," said Winnie-the-Pooh. "Don't you agree Rabbit?"

"Well. . . ah. . . oh, all right," muttered Rabbit. "I guess I like the old bouncy Tigger best, too."

"Oh, boy!" shouted Tigger, and he bounced right on top of Rabbit. "Come on. I'm going to teach you all how to bounce." And Tigger and the others — even Rabbit — bounced off together.

Published by Gallery Books
A Division of W.H. Smith Publishers Inc.
112 Madison Avenue
New York, New York 10016.

Produced by
Twin Books
15 Sherwood Place
Greenwich, CT. 06830.

ISBN 0-8317-9470-4

Printed in Hong Kong

2 3 4 5 6 7 8 9 10